# Appleseed

The Life and Legacy of John Chapman

## Joshua Blair

# Contents

Introduction

Preface

1 He Shall Be Called John

2 A Time to Plant

3 Standing in the Gates

4 A Voice of One in the Wilderness

Illustrations

5 Put Your Hand to the Plow

6 The Valley of the Shadow of Death

Afterward: Children Shall Rise Up and Call You Blessed

Notes

A Note on the Type

Published by Magnum Veritas Productions, LLC

Copyright © 2016 by Joshua Blair

All rights reserved. This is the property of Joshua Blair and no part of this book may be reproduced, copied, used, or distributed in any form without express written permission.

ISBN: 978-0-9982530-0-8

# Dedication

The first fruits of my literary work is dedicated to my Savior, God, and King, Jesus Christ.

# Special Thanks

To my amazing family: Papa, Mama, and Caleb for their immense patience and encouragement. Your guidance and faith has meant more to me than I can say.

Boatloads of gratitude to my inestimable cousin, Jessica Fry, for her professional advice and time spent throughout this project.

To Apple for their marvelous computers and software.

Also, many thanks to the musicians who helped me through the long hours of writing; Beethoven, Kenny G, Hans Zimmer, and the rest.

A special note of thanks to Robert Price for his thorough research behind the book *Johnny Appleseed: Man and Myth*. It has been an invaluable aid to every subsequent Appleseed chronicler, including this one.

I also would like to thank my illustrious and eccentric relative, without whom I would be at a loss for words.

Many thanks to Urbana University, Urbana, Ohio, without whom this book would be far shorter and less interesting. Incidentally, they request that I say, "Permission to use content from Robert Price's book, *Johnny Appleseed: Man and Myth* given by the Johnny Appleseed Foundation and Urbana University, Urbana, Ohio, Urbana, Ohio."

And finally, my deepest gratitude to God for His innumerable blessings to me and guidance throughout this process.

# Introduction

Anyone who has written about John Chapman after the nineteenth century has had ample cause to complain vociferously about the lack of reliable source material. Most have done so, and I would like to take a moment to add my list of grievances to an already lengthy one.

It is inevitable that as a character becomes a legend, those who knew him, or knew of him, develop an increasingly inflated and inaccurate memory. In the case of Johnny Appleseed, there emerges such a confounding web of fallacious and contradictory statements, that the coveted truth often appears to be entirely allusive.

What makes matters worse is that tall tales, mythical legends, and falsehoods did not wait to emerge until after Chapman's death; they were already prevalent in the primary source documentation. There are at least two reasons for this: the sheer magnitude of oddities surrounding John Chapman in real life which grew with retelling, and the exaggerated storytelling of Chapman, himself. He was not a quiet man, and it is doubtful whether he always adhered rigidly to the truth. This makes it very difficult to sort through what is and what is not the truth.

What is required is an historian of boundless patience and integrity to plumb the depths of this mess and begin strand by strand, to untangle the knots.

In 1954, Robert Price accepted the challenge and published *Johnny Appleseed: Man and Myth* laying down once and for all the most thorough, accurate, and authoritative biography on John Chapman to date.

While I relied heavily on Dr. Price's research, I also made use of other sources, including some primary source documentation which is, hopefully somewhat reliable.

I should also mention in passing, that I have kept any misspellings or grammatical errors in the primary sources the way it was written, and will henceforth avoid the use of unsightly "[sic]s".

If I were to lay out only that which was scientifically proven to be true beyond the shadow of a doubt, the result would be either a very small and boring paragraph, or else a patch-work quilt of unsightly caveats and qualifications. In my position, I'm forced to take some statements on faith.

While what follows is the truth as close as I can gather, it may still contain some erroneous statements. The only ones who hold the final key to the story of John Chapman are the apple trees he planted, and they have been regrettably silent for quite some time.

# Preface

Authors tend to have a number of reasons for writing a book, and want to communicate those reasons to their readers, who tend to not care. This conflict of interests has been neatly resolved by the invention of the preface, in which the author can get his numerous reasons off his chest, and which the reader can conveniently skip. In continuing this tradition, I will give my reasons for writing this book under the delusion that some absent-minded reader may accidentally mistake this preface for the first chapter and read it.

I don't write primarily because I enjoy it, or because I always wanted to be a writer when I grew up. I write because there are important ideas that I want to communicate to people so that we may all learn to live more fully and intentionally.

In this book, I seek to emphasize the principles and beliefs around which John Chapman lived his life. I want to get inside his head and tell the world what really mattered to him. By showing strengths of character to emulate, weaknesses to avoid, principles to embrace, and stories to remember, I hope to benefit all those who desire to "live deep and suck out all the marrow of life."

At rock bottom, John Chapman was a man who lived what he believed. Everything he did sprang out of the fertile ground of his beliefs. In our culture, we are used to giving mental assent to ideas without ever allowing them to influence the way we live. Our brains are full of philosophical and religious beliefs that contradict our daily actions and thereby deprive ourselves and those around us of the practical outflowing of those very ideas. We have a great need to return to an intentional lifestyle that is radically centered around what we believe.

That's what John Chapman did, and that's why his story needs to be told.

"Even if I knew that tomorrow the world would go to pieces, I would still plant my apple tree."

- Martin Luther

*Chapter 1*

# He Shall Be Called John

John Chapman is remembered as one of the most gentle, peaceful men to walk the earth. It is almost fitting, therefore, that he was born in one of the least peaceful states in one of the least peaceful years in American history. In 1774, the small town of Leominster, Massachusetts, was caught up in the wave of defiance that would soon mount into outright revolt against England. Thanks to Samuel Adams's tireless efforts in nearby Boston, the state of Massachusetts had become the epicenter of colonial dissent during the years leading up to the War for American Independence.

The Mayflower incident had caused some feathers to be ruffled, but discord between England and her colonies subsided when the Crown allowed the Separatists to worship freely in the new land. For almost one hundred fifty years, England and her American colonies enjoyed a mutually beneficial economic relationship. But after the French and Indian War of 1763, in which England saved her colonies from the French, England's war chest began to look rather sparse, and her national debt had risen to unsettling heights.

In view of this financial drain, the English put their crowned heads together and enacted the Sugar Act in 1764 to raise money from the American colonies. Prime Minister George Grenville had the dubious honor of proposing this tax plan. The political leaders in England were surprised to discover that the colonists vehemently objected to the three penny tax.*

From this point on, relations between England and her colonies steadily deteriorated. Bostonians, led by Samuel Adams, spearheaded the protest against the Sugar Act and the precedent of "taxation without representation". But it was, after all, a small tax and the dissent might have withered had it not been for the ill-advised Quartering and Stamp Acts of 1765.

These acts were also passed under Grenville who had remarkably failed to learn his lesson. The Quartering Act forced colonists to house British soldiers in their homes to alleviate the financial burden from the English. To add salt to the wound, the Stamp Act was passed a few months later which put a tax on newspapers, licenses, and other legal documents, in order to pay for the presence of the British soldiers. Newspapers and pamphlets were the colonies' main source of anti-British propaganda, and predictably, they churned out a steady stream of protests.

Boston, home of the Sons of Liberty, threw in a few well-organized riots for good measure; notably, an effigy of the Massachusetts stamp distributor was hung on the Liberty Tree near Boston Common with the catchy jingle, "A goodlier sight who e'er did see? / A Stamp-Man hanging on a tree!"

Colonial grumbling flared into overt hostility with the Boston Massacre of 1770. By the fall of 1774, the famous Boston Tea Party, in response to England's Tea Act, was celebrating its first anniversary, and in only seven months, shots would be fired on Lexington Green.

But these political changes and the uncertainty of the future that they brought were mixed with the comforting constancy of things that would always remain the same. Autumn was nearing again, and the season brought with it the brisk winds and coloring leaves. After harvesting the last crops of the year, farm families were preparing for another long winter, and whatever happened to stamp distributors and rabble-rousers, snow would settle in by Christmas.

On September 26, 1774, John Chapman was born into the rapidly changing world. Hindsight reveals many signs as to the man Chapman would become. His name, for one thing, possessed a certain significance. John means "Jehovah has been gracious" and Chapman refers to a merchant or trader having to do with bartering, bargains, and property.** And it was apple-picking time in Leominster.

John was the second child born to Nathaniel and Elizabeth Chapman. His older sister, Elizabeth, was four years his senior. Nathaniel Chapman's thoughts about the changing political world can be deduced from his actions; only five days before John was born, the Worcester County convention, twenty miles away, voted for a complete reorganization of the district militia with all officers of the British Crown carefully removed. Every town in the county had been instructed to enlist one third of all privates between the ages of sixteen and sixty years to be ready to act at a minute's notice. John's father, Nathaniel Chapman, was one of these original minutemen.

Nathaniel set off to war in April 1775, when his son was only seven months old. He fought at Bunker Hill, and a couple of years later was with Washington's army in New York. Nathaniel became a Captain in the Continental Army, from which he was more or less discharged in 1780. While there is some moderately biased evidence to the contrary, the prevailing theory for his dismissal is the mismanagement of the military stores with which he had been entrusted. This lack of business acumen was evidently a permanent fixture of Nathaniel's character. A letter from his first wife shows a low state in their family economy, and the fact that he lived with his second wife and ten or more children in a tiny frame house years later, shows that his fortunes did not improve much in later years.

While his famous son would never be mistaken for a shrewd and wealthy businessman, he was not quite the naive, destitute bumpkin that legends would have it. He had, doubtless, inherited some of his father's financial naiveté, but had still managed to pick up enough business sense along the way to buy nearly three hundred acres of land and lease eight hundred more.

In 1776, when John was not yet two years old, his mother was expecting again and in frail health. Her husband was away fighting alongside General Washington, and knowing that she might not have long to live, it was her earnest desire to see him again. "She felt that she must inform Nathaniel of her serious plight; yet she would not alarm him unduly, for he had worries enough of his own. Still, if he were only with her in person, the awful fears would soften." On June 3, 1776, three weeks before giving birth, Elizabeth wrote a letter to her husband giving an intimate look into this window of time in the Chapman family:

Loving Husband,

These lines come with my affectionate regards to you hoping they will find you in health, tho I still continue in a very weak and low condition. I am no better than I was when you left me but rather worse, and I should be very glad if you could come and see me for I want to see you.

Our children are both well thro the Divine Goodness.

I have received but two letters from you since you want away - neither knew where you was till last Friday I had one and Sabathday evening after, another, and I rejoice to hear that you are well and I pray you may thus continue and in God's due time be returned in safety. I send this letter by Mr. Mullins and I hope it will reach you and I should be glad if you would send me a letter back by him.

I have wrote that I should be glad you could come to see me if you could, but if you cannot, I desire you should make yourself as easy as possible for I am under the care of a kind Providence who is able to do more for me than I can ask or think and I desire humbly to submit to His Holy Will with patience and resignation, patiently to hear what he shall see fit to lay upon me. My cough is somewhat abated, but I think I grow weaker. I desire your prayers for me that I may be prepared for the will of God that I may so improve my remainder of life that I may answer the great end for which I was made, that I might glorify God here and finally come to the enjoyment of Him in a world of glory, thro the merits of Jesus Christ.

Remember, I beseech you, that you are a mortall and that you must submit to death sooner or later and consider that we are always in danger of our spiritual enemy. Be, therefore, on your guard continually, and live in a daily preparation for death - and so I must bid you farewell and if it should be so ordered that I should not see you again, I hope we shall both be as happy as to spend an eternity of happiness in the coming world which is my desire and prayer.

So I conclude by subscribing myself, your
Ever loving and affectionate wife

## Elizabeth Chapman

The letter has two postscripts. In the first, Elizabeth provides a quick summary of family and friends: Brother Zebedee, her father's family, the Johnsons, the Widow Smith's and Joshua Pierce's folks are all well. The second postscript gets briefly down to business and hints at the economic condition of the family:

"I have not bought a cow for they are very scarce and dear and I think I can do without, and I would not have you uneasy about it or about any money for I have as much as I need for the present."

"By the time this letter could have reached Nathaniel, the army in New York was anxiously engaged in the construction of entrenchments against an inevitable attack. Whether at any time during these weeks of critical preparation, Nathaniel was able to respond in person to his wife's... appeal, we do not know. The likelihood is small."

Elizabeth Chapman's "last brave letter to her husband was carefully treasured, in spite of Nathaniel's long soldiering and later remarriage, and was ultimately given into the safekeeping of his oldest child, Elizabeth, among whose descendants it came to light one hundred sixty-one years later."

John Chapman's mother, though weak in body, was strong in spirit. Her steadfast belief in God, religious fervor, and thoughtfulness of others shines through in her simple, yet eloquent letter. Elizabeth died when John was very young and it is unlikely that he could remember her in later years. Even so, all of the characteristics we know about her, with the exception of physical frailty, were notable aspects of his life.

On June 26, 1776, Elizabeth Chapman gave birth to her third child, a son, also named Nathaniel. Elizabeth grew progressively worse, and died on the 18th of July. The infant survived her by only a couple of weeks.

It is assumed that John and his sister, with their father off fighting the British and their mother no longer with them, were taken into the care of their mother's relatives in Leominster. Nathaniel returned to Massachusetts only after the war ended. In July, 1780, he married eighteen year old Lucy Cooley and moved his family to Longmeadow.

As is the case with so many, little is known of John's childhood. His thoughts on the war, whether he wanted it to last long enough for him to join, or to end soon so his father could come home, are lost to the annals of history. That he experienced a fair degree of education, perhaps in Longmeadow, can be inferred by his high level of literacy. Little else is known.

What is even more eery than the similarities between John Chapman and his parents, is the haunting resemblance between Chapman and ancestors further removed. Five generations before Nathaniel was Edward Chapman, recently landed from England, who on his death, bequeathed to his wife ten fruit trees. Edward's father-in-law, James Simons, built a frame house that stood for one hundred and fifty years, with the kind of tenacious longevity of John's own legacy. That frame house was one of the first houses built in what would become John's birthplace; the town of Leominster, Massachusetts.

As large of a role as John Chapman's ancestors had in shaping his character, the environment in which he grew may have played an even bigger part. The seeds sown by the American Revolution were the principles of liberty, independence, and what would become the thoroughly American ideal of individualism. He grew up in a predominately agrarian culture in which the family economy was the backbone of the national economy. It was an era of strong, hard-working men who knew how to be self-sufficient. It was a time of men like Daniel Boone and other pioneers, settlers, and trappers who went into the wilderness with little more than a rifle and their wit. It was an age of survivalists who eagerly took on the toughest challenges nature could throw at them.

After the American Revolution, the political climate began to relax and in quintessentially American fashion, the colonists began searching for the next adventure to undertake. The Louisiana Purchase and Lewis and Clark's expedition were several years away, but the colonies were already looking westward. It was the earliest dawn of westward expansion when settlers began moving to lands previously inhabited only by Indians and trappers. Was it this new spirit of adventure and taming of the wild that caused John Chapman to leave Longmeadow, or did it have more to do with him getting kicked in the head by a horse? *** No one knows. As Robert Price noted, "Any boy's inspirations are elusive, especially after a century and a half."

Suddenly, when he was twenty-three years old, John Chapman disappeared from Massachusetts and showed up in northern Pennsylvania on the Allegheny plateau. His preparations and reasons for leaving Leominster are lost to time. From our perspective, he materialized, as it were, out of nowhere. Some accounts suggest that he left home with his half-brother, Nathaniel, which is entirely possible.

Younger brothers have historically been inclined to follow their older brothers in practically any endeavor from flying to politics.

While his inspirations are no longer known, John Chapman's plans for what he would do in Pennsylvania would not be left to the imagination. He was about to plant his first nursery and earn his place in the pantheon of American legends.

*Chapter 2*

# A Time to Plant

By all accounts, John Chapman was an unusually-dressed character, even for the early frontier. Physically, he looked comparatively normal. One acquaintance described him as "a small man, wiry and thin in habit. His cheeks were hollow; his face and neck dark and skinny from exposure to the weather. His mouth was small; his nose small and turned up quite so much as apparently to raise his upper lip. His eye was dark and deeply set in his head, but searching and penetrating."

He would have looked perfectly normal, in fact, had it not been for his odd taste in clothes. There is hardly a first-hand account of Chapman that does not mention, at some point and to varying degrees of exaggeration, his dubious fashion sense. So many acquaintances discussed his attire, that clothing is one of the few things remembered about Chapman two hundred years later. Notably the bare feet and the mush pot hat.

"Generally, even in the coldest weather, he went barefooted, but sometimes, for his long journeys, he would make himself a rude pair of sandals; at other times he would wear any cast-off foot-covering he chanced to find - a boot on one foot and an old brogan or a moccasin on the other. His dress was generally composed of cast-off clothing, that he had taken in payment for apple-trees; and as the pioneers were far less extravagant than their descendants in such matters, the homespun and buckskin garments that they discarded would not be very elegant or serviceable."

Anyone who had the good fortune to bump into Chapman seemed to remember something about how he looked or how he was dressed. Another acquaintance states that "he was frequently seen with shirts, pants, and a kind of a long tailed coat of tow-linen then much worn by the farmers. This coat was a device of his own ingenuity and in itself a curiosity. It consisted of one width of the coarse fabric, which descended from his neck to his heels. It was without collar. In this robe were cut two arm holes into which were placed two straight sleeves."

Most people today, if they even remember Johnny Appleseed as a real figure in history, think of him as a naive bumpkin wearing a pot on his head. Those whose knowledge of Chapman goes beyond the Disney cartoon may recall that he also wore a coat made out of a coffee sack. Unfortunately, both the mush pot hat and coffee sack coat seem to be products of legend more than truth, but lacking these accouterments did not go far in normalizing Chapman's appearance.

After describing Chapman in the usual way (thin frame, dark hair, etc.), David Ayres added this description of the man whom he met on a number of occasions: "He slept on the floor on an old blanket. His old slipshod shoes were untidy looking and he seemed to care very little about his person. I never heard of his being sick."

There are many differing reports of Chapman that all describe him in loosely the same way, and almost all contradict each other on minor points. Sometimes he wears shoes and sometimes he is barefoot. One night, he sleeps on the floor and the next, he sleeps outside. The fact is, Chapman truly didn't care what he wore, which often led him to wear anything he came across on his journey: threadbare coats, heterogenous footwear, and whatever he found to fit the contours of his head. At a time when most settlers were seen wearing warm, sturdy clothes, John Chapman could be seen wearing literally anything.

Chapman had been residing near the Susquehanna River in late 1797, when he suddenly decided to cross the Appalachian mountains into the Allegheny Plateau of Northern Pennsylvania. In November of that year as he began his journey, the region was experiencing a pleasant Indian summer. But, as is often the case, the fair weather was short-lived. It wasn't long before he was probably wishing he had started a trifle sooner. In all its fury, winter rushed in, piling snow three feet high on the level. In nearby Philadelphia in November alone, it snowed more than three times the average amount. And the four and a half inches of rain didn't help.

Chapman was evidently unprepared for this. He had packed just enough provisions to make the trip, and in his exceptional mind, this did not include footwear. Being barefoot became something of a tradition of his over the years, but in the present case, it was more dangerous than anything. The heavy snows meant frostbite and worse if something wasn't done quickly. Improvising with the available resources, he ripped off part of his coat and bound it around his feet to serve in the place of shoes. The Pennsylvania slopes generously furnished beech trees whose long, flexible branches afforded Chapman another form of protection. Cutting some of these branches, he made them pliable through a process of heating them by a fire which he somehow managed to start, and then weaving them into a pair of snowshoes. Attaching them to his cloth-bound feet with strips of bark, he continued his journey. By about the first of December, he arrived at a small campsite that would eventually become the city of Warren, Pennsylvania.

Remarkable as this demonstration of quick-thinking and self-sufficiency was, this small episode in Chapman's life was typical of the kind of men America produced at the time. If settlers weren't skillful, knowledgable, and hard-working, they were typically dead. The treacherous wilderness of the American frontier built men who were even tougher, and could thrive in hostile environments.

John spent that winter scouting the area around the Allegheny River. In his pack, he carried a small quantity of apple seeds. When winter thawed into spring, he chose a spot on the Big Brokenstraw, a river that flows into the Allegheny six miles below Warren, and began planting his first apple nursery.

Nobody knows why Chapman chose this particular spot; certainly the population of settlers had nothing to do with it. There were only four people living in Warren at the time, and in ten years, one of them would leave to raft logs from the Allegheny all the way to New Orleans.

It's hard to imagine that the dedication of one's life to the planting of apple trees is anything but quaint. But in Chapman's day, apples weren't a nonessential frill or a pleasant snack to the early settlers. They were a fast-growing, versatile crop that provided for many of the urgent needs of frontier families.

Apples could be made into sauces, apple butter, and cider, cooked with almost any dish, and eaten right off the tree. In typical pioneer fashion, settlers also found a way to make it into an alcoholic beverage used liberally in the interests of hospitality. "Almost as important, fruit trees were also a frequent legal stipulation of land ownership."

They produced a steadily-increasing crop within five years on the outside, which is a relatively turn-around time. The trees were easily planted and once started, nurseries did not require constant, tender care. This would prove to be an important element in Chapman's method of working.

But Chapman's vision went far beyond increasing the number of apple trees in the midwest. He was actively involved in helping pioneers and settlers and "preparing a way in the wilderness for the men and women who would develop America." Settlers moving out west were able to set up their farms and establish homes much quicker with nurseries already waiting for them. Perhaps there was also a poetic inspiration for his planting. It is said that "he would describe the growing and ripening fruit as such a rare and beautiful gift of the Almighty with words that became pictures, until his hearers could almost see its manifold forms of beauty present before them."

For all of his accomplishments, Chapman was not the first person to introduce apples to the Midwest nor was he the first to set up a seedling apple tree business in the area. Ebenezer Zane, Rufus Putnam, and Jacob Nessley are just a few of the long-forgotten names of apple tree planters in the early American frontier days. But "no other orchardist planted as many nurseries as did John, and no other orchardist located his nurseries so carefully, always just ahead of the first settlers in an area and frequently just where a new center of population would spring up."

Today the common method for planting apple trees is by grafting; the result is a much more predictable, healthy apple tree with better fruit. One never knows what will spring up from a pile of seeds, and the practice of growing trees from seeds is now considered whimsical if not downright backward. Though grafting was a common practice in Chapman's day, his method of extensive travel all but prohibited the practice. Grafting would have required him carrying entire trees (albeit little ones) across great distances instead of several bags containing hundreds of apple seeds each.

It is even possible that he had a religious reason for not grafting. One source reported that "he denounced as absolute wickedness all devices of pruning and grafting, and would speak of the act of cutting a tree as if it were a cruelty inflicted upon a sentient being." All things considered, Chapman opted for the seedling method.

Thanks to the creative efforts of illustrators and animators, we think of Johnny Appleseed as a quaint bumpkin who lived closer to nature than to his fellow man. To his contemporaries, he was neither quaint nor reclusive. To them, he was someone who contributed a great service to them personally, and to the entire unfolding history of America's westward expansion. This was due, in large part, to the distinctive feature of Chapman's nursery business: his ability to move with the edge of the frontier. Other nurserymen had families, cabins, and other ties to the land that would not allow them to adjust their lives to the speed required by the expanding frontier. And as far as we know, none of them ever tried.

Chapman, on the other hand, never settled down in one location for long. He was always on the move, and this lifestyle meshed perfectly with the quickly changing scene of the westward frontier. Many historians have commented on Chapman's amazing knack for predicting where the next burst of western expansion would occur. When frontier families arrived, they often found a nursery planted by John Chapman waiting for them.

To stay routinely one step ahead of the frontier required an array of transportation methods. Most often, he chose the least likely option, traveling barefoot, often in the company of a horse or mule carrying his sacks of apple seeds.

One very early settler in 1806 saw him on the Ohio River "with two canoes lashed together... transporting a load of apple seeds to the Western frontier, for the purpose of creating orchards on the farthest verge of white settlements. With his canoes, he passed down the Ohio to Marietta, where he entered the Muskingum, ascending the stream of that river until he reached the mouth of the Walbonding, or White Woman Creek, and still onward, up the Mohican, into the Black Fork, to the head of navigation, in the region now known as Ashland and Richland counties, on the line of the Pittsburg and Fort Wayne Railroad, in Ohio. A long and toilsome voyage it was, as a glance at the map will show, and must have occupied a great deal of time, as the lonely traveler stopped at every inviting spot to plant the seeds and make his infant nurseries."

John acquired the seeds for planting his nurseries from cider-presses in Western Pennsylvania to which he regularly returned whenever he ran out. Generally, he transported them on foot, though as the story of the canoe voyage shows, he was not opposed to using other methods to cart them across the many frontier miles. The sacks he used to carry apple seeds were leather, one of the few materials aside from his feet that were able to withstand the long trips through dense forests and underbrush.

The land in which Chapman moved and planted was not the pleasant plains with neatly pruned hedges that it is today. It was an uncharted forest full of thick underbrush, thorns, bristles, and nettles of every kind. It was also replete with dangers of a more animalistic kind, and any pioneer needed strength of mind, nerve, and body to survive for even a short period of time. Venomous snakes and other reptiles hid in the grass to such a degree that one settler went on record as having killed more than two hundred rattlesnakes in one season. Settlers, like fishermen, are not always sticklers for the truth, but the obvious fact remains that there was no lack of rattlesnakes slithering around at the time.

Frontiersmen used cabins to protect against the elements, rifles to protect against hostile Indians, bears, and wolves, and much foot and leg protection to guard against the venomous inhabitants of the underbrush. But through this cornucopia of hell, John Chapman happily shouldered his bag of apple seeds and walked serenely and barefoot, planting his nurseries. Maybe there was something to the stories he told of God's providential protection after all. There is no human explanation for how he was able to survive as long as he did, alone and unprotected in the wilderness.

When planting his nurseries, it was Chapman's custom to clear an area, plant his seeds, and build a rough, make-shift fence around it. As the trees grew, he kept a periodic eye on them, maintaining and repairing the nursery as needed whenever passing through on his journeys.

Chapman's modus operandi in these early days was to squat on the land without bothering to lease, buy, or even acquire a written agreement from the owner. He simply moved in, planted, and moved out. In a few years, settlers arrived to find a thriving apple orchard from whence they transplanted trees to start their own nurseries.

As another tribute to his hardiness (if another one were needed) an early historian of John Chapman's wrote this: "All his work was done by hand, he never worked a horse or other animal, excepting in transporting his luggage from one point to another." "It also appears that Johnny was in the habit of making other plantings wherever he happened to be in his wanderings, perhaps at the home of a farmer who gave him lodging for the night or simply in a natural clearing in the woods, no matter who owned the land."

Regardless of land ownership, it was Chapman himself who always did the work in clearing land and planting and tending his nurseries. His was a hardy nature and many and varied are the stories of Chapman's fortitude. According to the first known written record of him, he allegedly thawed ice with his bare feet.* It has also been reported that in his effort to amuse boys, "he stuck pins in his feet and walked on red-hot coals. He seems to have been impervious to most pain." His method of treating cuts was both unorthodox and painful; he would sear the cut with a red-hot iron, and then treat it as a burn.

For all of this, Chapman was not a masochist; he didn't endure pain for its own sake, but for the practical benefit of others. One of his acquaintances said he could do as much work in one day as most men did in two, splitting rails and girdling trees. He was known to help settlers in building cabins or fixing fences, and in all of these activities, Chapman worked as hard, and often harder, than everyone else.

His toughness was as much a result of his religious beliefs as his inborn physical strength. He reportedly slept on the floor because he didn't believe there were beds in heaven, so what was the point getting used to them on earth? And of course, there is the oft-repeated story of how he walked barefoot in the snow after inadvertently trampling and killing a worm while wearing shoes. Chapman was known far and wide for his regard of all life – human and animal – and this came, as did most things, from his belief in God and God's creation of life. Misguided, strange, or superstitious as some of his religious beliefs might have been, they were never just intellectual exercises. Chapman was fully committed to living out what he believed, no matter how uncomfortable the result.

Chapman's stomach was as legendary as his feet. He often ate outside and sometimes lived for periods of time on the same type of food. "He frequently lived on fruit and nuts in their season. He once hired a young man to help him a little about his work, and at meal time he took him to his den and set out a quantity of Black Walnuts for him to make his meal out of them. To this the young man demurred and finally left in disgust."

While the fortitude of his stomach afforded him the ability to eat a wider array of food than many of his associates, it, like everything in his life, was a product of his faith. Chapman thought it was a sin to kill animals, even for food, and believed that everything a man needed to survive came from the ground. Settlers are known to live with few and arduously acquired resources, and as such, are not known to waste, but Chapman took this tendency to a whole new level. Once as he was passing a cabin, he noticed some pieces of bread in a slop bucket for pigs. He retrieved the bread for his own lunch, and told the cabin's housewife that since God had graciously given certain things for the provision of mankind, it would be a terrible waste not to use them for their intended purpose.

All of Chapman's strength was needed in the harsh world in which he lived. Early settlers were often fighting, swearing, getting drunk, and meting out punishment with harsh brutality. It was not unheard of for a man to be beaten within an inch of his life for stealing a handful of knickknacks. Drunken brawls occasionally ended with manslaughter and few frontiersman lived to a ripe old age.

In this environment, Chapman proved himself countless times to be one of the most physically powerful men on the frontier. There were few boastful stories from settlers that matched up with Chapman's true-to-life feats of stamina. He was renowned for his strength, but perhaps even more for his humanity. Chapman, in all his kindness and gentleness, stands out in distinct relief from the unfeeling backdrop of his times.

His kindness with other people, often at his own expense, was legendary. "On one occasion, in an unusually cold November, while he was traveling barefooted through mud and snow, a settler who happened to possess a pair of shoes that were too small for his own use forced their acceptance upon Johnny, declaring that it was sinful for a human being to travel with naked feet in such weather. A few days afterward the donor was in the village that has since become the thriving city of Mansfield and met his beneficiary contentedly plodding along with his feet bare and half frozen. With some degree of anger he inquired for the cause of such foolish conduct, and received for reply that Johnny had overtaken a poor, barefooted family moving Westward, and as they appeared to be in much greater need of clothing than he was, he had given them the shoes."

Despite having very little money, he gave much of it away in his travels. Chapman could be accused of many things, but being miserly was not one of them. He was known to give away as much as fifty dollars, quite a large amount at the time, to a settler or family in need.

On another occasion, he bought six plates at a store in Mansfield. When a curious bystander asked him why he wanted six, Chapman joked that with six plates he wouldn't need to wash any of them for a week. In reality, he had bought them for a poor settler's family who didn't have any plates, and as always, when he gave them the plates, he accepted nothing in return.

Other times, when he had nothing else to give, Chapman gave his precious apple trees. Some say he left a standing order to those who maintained his nurseries in his absence to give away trees without charge to families or persons in need.

One story, in particular, shows Chapman's generosity. The Hunter children, all nine of them, lost both parents when David, the oldest, was only sixteen years old. Without any money and needing to provide for his siblings, David was between the proverbial rock and a hard place. One day he chanced to meet John Chapman who sat down and talked with him about how things were going. Seeing his situation, Chapman supplied David with about sixty trees for which no payment was ever asked. In time, David Hunter was able to grow the size of his orchard to ten times the original amount and establish a decent living for himself and his siblings.

While kind to adults, Chapman took a special interest in children. He made it a point to have strips of ribbon and colorful cloth, or other small presents to give to the children he met in his travels. Whenever he ate with a family, he first made sure the children had enough before helping himself. He was sympathetic and understanding to young children throughout his life, winning many young friends who remembered him and the little kindnesses he paid them for years to come. Like the God he served, Chapman suffered the little children to come to him.

His compassion reached even to animals. As he traveled, Chapman kept an eye out for lame or otherwise debilitated horses, and nursing them back to health, gave them away to settlers who shared his humanitarian nature. But his care for animals went beyond just the nice, harmless, and beneficial ones like horses. As one story goes, he found a wolf caught in a trap and, much to the trapper's dismay, released it and nursed it back to health. Afterward, the wolf never left his side, following him like a dog. Whether or not this story is true is anyone's guess, but considering Chapman, it's not far-fetched.

As with everything, his kindness to animals came directly from his religious beliefs. He believed it was wrong to take the life of any animal, and said that since God is the Creator of life, all life belongs to Him to take when He sees fit. He also maintained that since we can not give life to any animal, we should not take it, either.

In fact, it's almost impossible to find anyone who did not benefit from Chapman's kindness. Animals, harmless and otherwise, settlers young and old, and even Indians who were often less than friendly, knew that Chapman was different. To the Indians, Chapman was the "great medicine man" due, in part, to his eccentric appearance and imperviousness to pain, which was even greater than their own. But the title was really won by his prodigious knowledge of the medicinal quality of herbs and other plants on the frontier which he used to help settlers and Indians alike. Even during times of revenge and slaughter between Indian and settler, Chapman was trusted by both and moved between the two camps unmolested, planting apple trees. Aside from one minor instance in which some tribesmen stole a handful of his ponies, Chapman was never in danger from the Indians who respected him almost as much as the settlers did.

This would prove to be invaluable in the role he was about to play. Up to this point, the wilderness had been sparsely populated by rough, drunken settlers, stone-faced Indians, and a kind, wandering apple tree planter. But the uneasy relations between settlers and Indians were about to erupt and the strange wanderer would play a significant part in preventing the clash from becoming a massive tragedy.

*Chapter 3*

# Standing in the Gates

The Prophet began to dream. For years, Native American Indians had suffered at the hands of white men from the east. The rapidly expanding frontier experienced its share of growing pains, and in most cases, it was the Indians who received the pain. Frontiersmen cut down large sections of forests to plant crops and build houses. They shot and trapped wild animals, in time, pushing some species to near extinction. Frontiersmen were often unjust and crooked in their dealings with the Indians whom they viewed as inferior. And frontiersmen brought friends from the east who did the same.

The great Indian chief, Tecumseh, was not one to take this injustice lying down, but in order to fight the invaders, he needed to gain the crucial support of the numerous local tribes; the Senecas, Ottawas, Shawnees, and Wyandots. The answer to Tecumseh's dilemma came in the form of his brother, Tenskwatawa, known among his people as "the Prophet."

The Prophet brought spiritual support to Tecumseh's military vision. The Prophet gained credence and loyalty from the Indians through his ability to foresee supernatural events. He predicted the solar eclipse in 1806, a prediction that had been derided by the Indiana Territorial Governor, William Henry Harrison. The Prophet told the Indians that he had received revelations from the Great Spirit about the future of the tribes.

His was a utopian vision of unified Indian tribes that would throw off the oppressive yoke of the white man. Conveniently, this was also Tecumseh's vision for pushing the settlers back east. This coalition would be driven spiritually by the dreams of the Prophet, emotionally by the desire for a happy future, and physically by Tecumseh's military strategy.

Tecumseh and the Prophet chose their headquarters in northern Indiana along the Tippecanoe River to integrate and strengthen the coalition. Whether or not they would ultimately succeed, they were a force to be reckoned with and a formidable threat to the settlers' safety on the frontier. There was going to be trouble again between the natives and settlers, and in the midst of it all, was an unlikely character who was about to play a pivotal role in how the situation unfolded.

Early on, John Chapman developed a reputation for gentleness and kindness that was the polar opposite to the early settler's typical behavior.

One well-circulated story had to do, once again, with animals. It seems Chapman was mowing with a hand-scythe when a snake slithered out of the grass and bit him. As probably most would have done, Chapman killed the snake with the scythe. It was not long before his humanitarian conscience pricked him, and he was filled with remorse. With tears in his eyes, he said, "Poor fellow! He only touched me, and I killed him in the heat of my ungodly passion!" His kindness to animals was legendary, and included everything from horses and bears to snakes and insects.

"He would often examine the old wood that he was about to put on the fire and if a worm or ants or any living thing was found connected with it, he would either knock them all off or throw the wood to one side."

On another occasion, Chapman was preparing to spend the night outside and built a fire to keep warm. But he noticed that the light from the fire attracted a large number of mosquitoes and other insects, many of which died in the smoke. Anyone else would have been happy about this situation, but not Chapman. He quickly extinguished the fire with a bucket of water, saying, "God forbid that I should destroy any of the creatures He has created for my own comfort." Whether or not mosquitoes were created for man's comfort is a matter of opinion.

Another tale has it that he was helping some settlers build a road through the woods. As they were working, someone inadvertently harmed a hornet's nest and one of the hornets found its way into Chapman's clothes. It stung him repeatedly, but instead of killing it, he gently and patiently extricated it. Perhaps he remembered the incident of the snake and didn't want to repeat his error. After the angry insect was finally removed, the other men working with him asked why he hadn't squashed it. He said, "It would be wrong to kill it, since the poor thing had not intended any harm." What the insect's intentions were is also a matter of opinion.

Some said that Chapman never killed an animal for food, preferring to take his nourishment from the soil. He claimed the soil produced all that was needed to sustain human life. For the wellbeing of animals, Chapman was willing to deny himself warmth, comfort, and as another tale has it, even a place to sleep.

One snowy night, Chapman was alone in the forest without any protection. He was about to sleep in a hollow log with a fire burning on the other side to stay warm, when he discovered that the log was already occupied by a mother bear and her cubs. Feeling sorry for them, Chapman left them in possession of the log and spent the night in the open air on the snow.

One tired writer commenting on this incident said dryly, "that to leave a mother bear and her cubs undisturbed was the most obvious of common sense." Knowing Chapman, his night in the snow may have been a combination of both common sense and kindness.

It was, in large part, due to this gentleness with humans and animals alike, that Chapman became one the few people to earn the trust of both settlers and Indians. Henry Howe, in his prodigious "Historical Collections of Ohio", remarked that "He was careful not to injure any animal, and thought hunting morally wrong. He was welcome everywhere among the settlers, and was treated with great kindness even by the Indians."

By 1812 after Chapman's stint in Mansfield and Mount Vernon, he moved north to the Lake Erie watershed. This would become the location of one of his greatest services to the pioneers and one that would be forever linked with the growing Appleseed legend. The Indian incident, charged with uncertainty and anxiety, had its fair share of false starts.

The few families living in the area, knowing how serious a threat the Indians were, enlisted the aid of John Chapman as a lookout. This was, in one respect, an unusual choice because time did not weigh heavily on Chapman's hands. Aside from his constant travels in transporting apple seeds, and his work in planting and maintaining orchards, he was known to constantly lend his neighbors a hand in erecting houses or repairing fences. To this was now added a fair share of scouting and reconnaissance work. Chapman cheerfully accepted these added duties and made a weekly report to the frontier families of any developments.

He was living at the time with a settler named Caleb Palmer. Nearby (according to frontier standards) was another settler by the name of Woodcock. It was agreed among them that in case of an Indian attack, one of them would fire a gun as a signal, and to avoid confusion, none of them were to fire a gun under any other circumstances.

One day when Chapman and Palmer were working in the field, they heard a gunshot come from the direction of Woodcock's cabin. This was followed by two more shots as fast as a man could load. They immediately ran back to their cabin and prepared to beat a precipitous retreat to warn the other settlers down the river. But before leaving, Chapman decided to take a look around the Woodcock cabin. Donning Indian garb and taking a gun, he headed to the scene of the gunshots. Palmer, it was decided, would wait until Chapman returned to tell him how the situation stood.

Three agonizing hours passed for Palmer without a sign of his friend. Racked with doubts and fear, Palmer accordingly took his gun and edged his way cautiously toward Woodcock's cabin. He was close to the area when he saw a shadowy form moving through the bushes. Seeing what looked like the red leggings of an Indian, Palmer breathed slowly and waited to get a clearer view of his antagonist. When the form appeared again, he leveled his gun and took steady aim. At which point, John Chapman stepped through the foliage and came into view.

The matter was soon explained. A deer had had the misfortune of putting in an appearance near Woodcock's cabin, and the settler couldn't resist taking a shot at it. When Chapman discovered what had happened, he promptly forgot about Palmer and in his neighborly way, helped Woodcock skin and dress the deer. Afterward, he took a piece of the venison and leisurely made his way back to Palmer's, where he was subsequently mistaken for an Indian and almost shot. There was a collective sigh of relief, but the real danger was only postponed.

Everyone was feeling skittish, as evidenced by another false alarm, this one on the twenty-first of August. It was Chapman who sounded the alarm, and soon entire families, including the Reverend McIntyre, who would later be known as one of Chapman's rivals in religious discussions, were cutting their way through the drenched and tangled underbrush to meet each other and determine the safest course of action. A special express brought the news that two thousand Indians led by the British had overrun several small settlements and were marching on to Sandusky. This note did not alleviate the general anxiety.

Confusion ran rampant; no one knew what the situation was or where they were going, or what was happening to the homes they had hurriedly left. They decided the safest course was to make their way as quickly as possible to Mansfield, even though they had to travel at night. Caleb Palmer served as the guide and they began their strenuous journey at nine o'clock in the evening. Despite the darkness, confusion, and the Huron which was full to the banks, they managed to arrive in Mansfield the next morning. The few cabins there didn't offer the needed protection, so they proceeded south twenty miles to Fredericktown.

Rumors met them the entire way of murderous and pillaging Indians and British who were decimating the countryside and killing settlers. After awhile, though, facts slowly emerged. What had happened was nine boats containing American prisoners released by the British at Detroit had arrived at a landing place on the shore of Lake

Erie. It was these boats that had been mistaken for the band of two thousand Indians.

Despite the long, arduous journey at night through heavy rain, muddy paths, and matted underbrush, it was far better to be overly cautious than to die under a tomahawk. As the following incident showed, a little service in time of real danger could cause previous mistakes to be forgotten and "the boy who cried wolf" to be a hero.

An uneasy lull followed the turmoil of the false alarms, and for some time things quieted down. It was the proverbial calm before the storm.

One day, on a routine walk through the woods, Levi Jones, a merchant and whiskey supplier, was suddenly ambushed by Indians hiding behind fallen logs. They fired on him and Jones ran despite being hit. The Indians overtook him, stabbed and scalped him, and promptly fled. Some men working nearby heard the shots and the cries and quickly ran to warn the other settlers. Everyone immediately panicked again, and, as is typical in such situations, assumed that more settlers had been murdered than in fact, had been. The families nearby gathered together in the Mansfield blockhouse for the night as a safeguard against Indian raids. They knew more protection was needed, but the closest soldiers were miles away and no one knew when the Indians would attack again. Someone needed to go for help and warn the other inhabitants in the area who had yet to hear of Jones's death.

John Chapman volunteered to make the thirty mile journey to Mount Vernon, warning the settlers and bringing aid for those in the blockhouse.

Whether he made the journey on horseback or on foot is disputed. If a horse was available, he doubtless would have taken it, but in the hurried retreat to the blockhouse, horses might have been overlooked. If such was the case, it is likely that Chapman was the only frontiersman fit and willing enough to tackle the journey on foot as quickly as was needed. His feet, after all, were no strangers to adversity.

One report says that as he ran by cabins on his way to get reinforcements, he shouted, "The Spirit of the Lord is upon me, and he hath anointed me to blow the trumpet in the wilderness, and sound an alarm in the forest; for, behold, the tribes of the heathen are round about your doors, and a devouring flame followeth after them."

While the poetic and spiritual nature of the saying fits with the Appleseed legend, it is doubtful whether one as resourceful as Chapman would have unleashed such an unnecessary torrent of words.

In the end, Jones turned out to have been the only one killed by the Indians. The blockhouse tenants were unharmed and Chapman brought Captain Douglass and fifteen volunteer soldiers to Mansfield the next morning. In an anti-climactic sort of way, the reinforcements failed to run into Jones's murderers, and the Indian incident ended there. But settlers had been warned, harm had been averted, and the comforting sight of soldiers had all come about through the hand (or feet) of John Chapman.

He had been a guardian angel through this turbulent time, and the settlers would always be grateful for the service he had rendered. Settlers were never ones to let good deeds go unrewarded. William Henry Harrison was elected President of the United States largely on the strength of having defeated Tecumseh at Tippecanoe in 1811 and John Chapman would be forever immortalized as one of the heroes of the frontier for service rendered above and beyond the call of duty.

*Chapter 4*

# A Voice of One in the Wilderness

No life is divided into convenient little compartments. John Chapman's missionary work and religious beliefs were not a separate part of his life; they were the core of what tied his entire life work together.

Chapman followed the doctrines of Emmanuel Swedenborg. What is now termed Swedenborgianism, a mythic form of Christianity, was in Chapman's day, called the "New Church." Chapman was such an ardent believer in Swedenborgianism that the fact is mentioned in almost every account, contemporary or otherwise, written on his life; which is even more remarkable for the lack of consistency in describing almost every other area of his life.

While there are many finer, confusing points of Swedenborgianism, the two main doctrines teach that Jesus is God and followers must obey His commandments. It is also taught that if one lives a good life in accordance with the commands of God, God will accept one into heaven on the basis of one's goodness. Swedenborg taught that there was both a Heaven and a Hell; good people went to the one and bad people went to the other.

The doctrine that Jesus Christ is God was taken beyond the camp of orthodox Christianity by stating that instead of a Trinity, God was one person revealed in the person of Jesus Christ. This is referred to today as "Oneness Pentecostalism." However, as is typical with Swedenborg's teachings, there are added some impenetrable lines of thought that reflect a belief in the Trinity which somehow originated after creation.

While Swedenborg taught that Scripture was inspired by God, there is a strong belief in extra-biblical revelation. Swedenborg, himself, claimed inspiration for many of his writings. Concerning salvation, Swedenborg taught that man is being pulled by Hell to do bad and by Heaven to do good. This equilibrium was imbalanced in Hell's favor before Christ's coming so that no one could be saved. Christ came, it is taught, to balance the scale and give man free will to choose to do either good and go to Heaven, or bad and go to Hell.

These are the main doctrines of Swedenborgianism, though there are many other complex, minor teachings that cover a wide range of insignificant subjects.

While close in many points to what the Bible teaches, Swedenborgianism differs on several major points, ones which caused heated debates between New Church members and Protestants in Chapman's day. The two biggest differences are those of soteriology (the doctrine of salvation) and the doctrine of the Trinity.

Chapman was an adherent to both the teachings of the Bible and Swedenborg, and being literate and well-read in both, it's impossible to know which side of these doctrinal divides he favored. Further complicating matters, some of Chapman's beliefs don't seem to fall in line with either teachings. He "devoutly believed that the more he endured in this world the less he would have to suffer and the greater would be his happiness hereafter—he submitted to every privation with cheerfulness and content, believing that in so doing he was securing snug quarters hereafter." While this may go a long way in explaining his cheerful willingness to sleep on the floor, walk barefoot, and endure countless other inconveniences, it is a belief that is found in neither the Bible nor the teachings of Swedenborg. Such is also the case with the two female spirits he allegedly conversed with and who promised to be his wives in the afterlife so long as he abstained from marriage on earth. Where he got these ideas, no one knows. Maybe there's something in that story of the horse kick, after all.

Regardless of the doctrines he adhered to, what is certain is that everything Chapman did was a result of his religious beliefs. From practically his first appearance in Pennsylvania to his death in Indiana, it was Chapman's religion that was the driving force of his life.

It is generally a source of surprise for historians to find that the first mention of John Chapman's missionary work emerged, not on the American continent, but in England. This just proves the point that the events surrounding Chapman's life were never predictable. The report came from the *Society for Printing, Publishing and Circulating the Writings of Emanuel Swedenborg* in Manchester, England, on January 14, 1817, and details many aspects of Chapman's character, habits, and activities:

"There is in the western country a very extraordinary missionary of the New Jerusalem. A man has appeared who seems to be almost independent of corporeal wants and sufferings. He goes barefooted, can sleep anywhere, in house or out of house, and live upon the coarsest and most scantly fare. He has actually thawed the ice with his bare feet.

He procures what books he can of the New Church; travels into the remote settlements, and lends them wherever he can find readers, and sometimes divides a book into two or three parts for more extensive distribution and usefulness. This man for years past has been in the employment of bringing into cultivation, in numberless places in the wilderness, small patches (two or three acres) of ground, and then sowing apple seeds and rearing nurseries.

These become valuable as the settlements approximate, and the profits of the whole are intended for the purpose of enabling him to print all the writings of Emanuel Swedenborg, and distribute them through the western settlements of the United States."

The writings that he distributed were not always complete. "He was a constant reader and would often tear a Book in pieces to distribute as he passed through the country."

This custom sprang out of his lack of available material and was facilitated by his habit of travel. Chapman had a back-and-forth method of traveling across the frontier: he gathered apple seeds from cider presses in the east, planted nurseries as he moved west, and checked on them to maintain their condition when he went back east for more seeds. In this way, he often visited the same log-cabin several times in a year and was able to leave fresh fragments of books.

Through this system, several families spread out over a large area could eventually read the same book, even if Chapman only had one copy. Of course, Swedenborg is difficult enough to understand if read in chronological order and all at once. It is to be wondered how any of the frontier families could be expected to understand any of this fragmented reading, especially if they had the misfortune of receiving the last section first.

The Swedenborg writings that Chapman read and circulated were, at least in part, supplied by one of the few

New Church members in America, William Schlatter of Philadelphia. On May 4, 1817, Schlatter wrote the following to the pastor of the New Church society in Wheeling:

"...I have sent some books to Mr. Chapman, do you know him and has he received the Books, he travels about in Ohio and has much to do with appletrees; I am told he is a singular man but greatly in love with the New Church doctrines and takes great pains in deseminating them."

Accustomed to larger than life myths of John Chapman, it is amusing to hear the greatly understated facts that he is a "singular man" who "has much to do with appletrees." Mr. Schlatter, not given to exaggeration, was extravagant in his praise of Chapman's religious fervor, his love of the doctrines, and the great pains he took to disseminate them. These pains were rewarded.

Chapman was the only New Churchman (also called "receiver") in the Mansfield area when he arrived in 1813. In seven years, there were more; how many is not known, but a sufficient number to attract attention. In the twenty-five years following Chapman's arrival in Mansfield, Swedenborgian societies, albeit small ones, emerged in over ten counties in the surrounding area. These groups, it is generally acknowledged, owed their existence to the tireless evangelistic efforts of John Chapman.

It is possible that when he first arrived in the midwest, Chapman was the only active New Church evangelist in the area. Mr. Schlatter, in writing to Silas Ensign of Mansfield in November 1822, was characteristically understated in saying that "Mr. Chapman has no doubt been very instrumental in spreading the truth." As it stood, Chapman may have been the only one spreading the truth in many of his travels. "He always carried with him some work on the doctrines of Swedenborg with which he was perfectly familiar, and would readily converse and argue on his tenets, using much shrewdness and penetration."

A letter dated April 16, 1821 from Schlatter to Reverend John Clowes of Manchester, England sheds more light on Chapman's missionary service:

> "I have received a letter from a zealous member of the New Church, and one who appears most anxious to spread the doctrines of truth... He offers land for books but as our societies have no books on hand it is out of their power to supply him. It is my intention to send him a few books I had published.
> I enclose a copy of his letters that you may know something of his character. He is a singular man and our friend Mr. Condy who has conversed with him in Ohio states him to be intelligent and says the great object of his life appears to be to promote the doctrines. If some of the printing Societies or any of our friends have books to spare I think they will be faithfully distributed by Mr. Chapman."

Aside from again referring to him as being "singular", Schlatter brought to light the invaluable addition that Chapman's great object in life was to promote the doctrines in which he believed. The trade he chose could hardly have been more fitting. As a wandering planter of apple trees, Chapman was able to cover a wide range in his evangelistic efforts. And his immensely beneficial provision of the trees would have made frontiersmen more receptive to hearing what he had to say. The offer of land for books is more clearly communicated in another letter, this one from a Daniel Thunn on May 15, 1821 to Margaret Bailey of Cincinnati:

"...To add something more to the New Church news, there is Mr. John Chapman near Wooster, Ohio, who wrote lately to Mr. Schlatter that he found an increase of Receivers all around his neighborhood and that they are spreading as far as Detroit, he proposed to make a Deed over to the New Church for a Quarter Section of Land and take payment in Books of the New Church. We contemplate how best to fulfill his wishes. This is the Appleseed man you certainly must have heard of, who goes around in the Country to plant Apple trees."

Mr. Thunn took it for granted that Margaret Bailey had heard of John Chapman. Perhaps they had spoken of him before, but this is not necessarily the case. Chapman was as famous while alive as he was many years after his death, when the legends had grown larger than the apple trees he planted.

Today, the practice of selling land in return for religious tracts is unheard of, and the practice didn't seem to have been any more prevalent in Chapman's day. That he would be willing to part with such a precious possession as virgin land in exchange for tracts shows in a practical light how his evangelistic efforts were, as Schlatter said, the great object of his life. Singular man, indeed.

On November 18, 1822, in another letter from the prolific pen of William Schlatter, it was reported that "Mr. Ensign says when he first went there, there was but one receiver and that was Mr. John Chapman, whom you must have heard me speak of, they call him John Appleseed out there." This was the first known mention of John Chapman's nickname and characteristic of other early titles, gives the name as "John Appleseed." The subsequent "Johnny" occurred only after Chapman died.

The small New Church community in America had much to say in favor of one who was soon to become their most famous member. On June 3-5, 1822, the Fifth General Convention of the New Churchmen in Philadelphia gave the following report on Chapman:

"...one very extraordinary missionary continued to exert, for the spread of divine truth his modest and humble efforts, which would put the most zealous members to the blush. We now allude to Mr. John Chapman, from whom we are in the habit of hearing frequently. His temporal employment consists in preceding the settlements, and sowing nurseries of fruit trees, which he avows to be pursued for the chief purpose of giving him an opportunity of spreading the doctrines throughout the western country.

In his progress, which neither heat nor cold, swamps nor mountains, are permitted to arrest, he carries on his back all the New Church publications he can procure, and distributes them wherever opportunity is afforded. So great is his zeal, that he does not hesitate to divide his volumes into parts, by repeated calls, enable the readers to peruse the whole in succession.

Having no family, and inured to hardships of every kind, his operations are unceasing. He is now employed in traversing the district between Detroit and the closer settlements of Ohio.

What shall be the reward of such an individual, where as we are told in holy writ, 'They that turn many to righteousness shall shine as the stars forever.' "

It is to be wondered whether Swedenborg's teachings, unfathomable to many, were understood at all by Chapman's often illiterate audience. But illiteracy and perplexing doctrine were only two of the obstacles in Chapman's way. One of the main forces with which he had to contend was the enormous amount of other religions swirling in the area at the time: "Never... has there been such a heterogenous mingling of sects and systems as that which surged through western Pennsylvania, Ohio, and Indiana from 1790 to 1850. Sabbatarians, Free-Will Baptists, Congregationalists, Bible Christians, Wesleyans, Old School and New School Presbyterians, Covenanters, Mennonites, Unitarians, Universalists, Adventists, Jerkers, Millerites, Friends, Restorationists, United Brethren, and Mormons."

Chapman met and engaged with all of these people in a similar way. After traveling all day, he would arrive at a cabin, which, in typical frontier hospitality, would be open to him. Depositing himself on the floor, he asked his hearers if they would like to hear "some news right fresh from heaven." Producing a Bible or well-worn Swedenborgian books, he would read aloud and expound on the reading to his hearers.

One family that often welcomed Chapman into their home was the Emry family, the patriarch of whom was a Baptist preacher. Soon after Emry arrived in Richland County in 1816, he heard of Chapman and invited him to stay at his house. Emry might have been one of the few people who was as eager to discuss religious themes as Chapman, himself. Emry learned, as others had, that Chapman was no ignorant fanatic, but one of the most well-learned and intelligent minds he would ever meet. Being a Baptist, he and Chapman had many long but charitable debates about the differences between their doctrines. The Emry cabin was always open to him, and Chapman often stayed there in later years.

Not all of those who disagreed with Chapman did so as agreeably as Emry. One of the more passionate, religious debaters Chapman met during his journeys was the Methodist Reverend James McIntyre.

The similarities between Chapman and McIntyre are stark and unsettling. Neither were formally taught in theology, and both seemed to have picked up their knowledge from books they found on their journeys. Both were tall and thin, with deep-set eyes, and both were famous for their eccentric dress. McIntyre wore homogenized tow-cloth garments: tow-cloth shirt and pantaloons, held up by a single suspender of the same material. And both men were barefoot.

To see two such similar religious zealots debating the finer points of Swedenborgian theology on the early frontier would have been an extraordinary sight.

In his biography of John Chapman, Robert Price tells several humorous anecdotes in the history of Chapman's religious debates on the frontier. It is a wonder that we still have the records of these conversations, however warped by the telephone game.

"He believed this world to be a type of the next, they said. The future world would have the same physical geography, the same phenomena of cold and heat, rains and snows, the same occupations of life, and the same emotions of love and hate, joy and sadness, and so on.

One favorite story turned the trick of the argument against John. A wag was interrogating him on the point of employments in the spiritual world:

"So you think man will follow the same occupations in Heaven?"

"I really do."

"Do people die in Heaven?"

"I think not."

"Then my occupation is gone," said the wag sadly, "for I am a grave-digger."

Usually, he was equal to the banter. Some Mansfield lawyers were rallying him on the same point:

"Mr. Chapman, what business will lawyers follow in Heaven?"

"The woe pronounced against them prevents their getting to that place."

"Then where will they go?"

"To Hell."

"And what will engage their attentions there?"

"Just what engages their attention here," - great suavity - "they will be placed in filth up to their knees, and will be striving forever to pitch it into each other's faces."

The lawyers proceeded to question the next witness.

The first Baptists around Perrysville sometimes held services in the White cabin near old Greentown. John was present one day and after the Reverend Otis had finished preaching, asked permission to make a few remarks:

"Are you a preacher?" Otis asked.

"I am a messenger sent before you into the wilderness."

"To what denomination do you belong?"

"I am a believer in the doctrines of Emanuel Swedenborg."

"Ah, indeed! But sir, I stand opposed to those doctrines."

"That's nothing strange, Mr. Otis," was Chapman's firm reply, "when we consider that your father, the devil, is opposed to them too. Children generally follow the teachings of their parents."

For all of his talking, Chapman was a good listener. When a preacher was giving a sermon, as periodically happened on the frontier, Chapman was often seen nearby, listening with rapt attention. He was similarly eager to read any religious pamphlets and books that he came across when staying at some hospitable cabin. Intelligent and thoughtful, he was always willing to hear what someone else had to say, though on one legendary occasion, he decided to put in his own two cents.

"Of all Johnny Appleseed's actual or mythical sectarian brushes, the "primitive Christian" incident has become by all odds the most famous. It has been carried on into the legend itself and is always told whenever the nature of John Chapman's mission is being discussed. It has been related so many times, in fact, that it has numerous variations, is set in many different parts of Ohio and Indiana, and several different frontier revivalists are named as the victim of the incident, including the great Peter Cartwright.

It was a Mansfield episode originally, however, and two separate testimonies identify the itinerant preacher who was responsible for it as Adam Payne, an illiterate fanatic, who went about the settlements, with long hair and long beard flying, calling himself "the Pilgrim" and exhorting the citizens to repent of their many sins and be saved.

Samuel Coffinbury remembered that Payne reached Mansfield the year the old courthouse was erected (1829 or 1830), blew a tin horn to announce his presence and preached to an audience sitting on the stones and timbers lying around the public square. John W. Dawson of Fort Wayne recalled Payne's appearing in that town a short time afterward in 1830, where he mounted a box on the northeast corner of Clinton and Columbia streets with the announcement, "Hear ye! Hear ye!" At the conclusion of his rant, John Chapman came forward out of the crowd and asked Payne if he remembered the "primitive Christian" of the incident in Mansfield a short time previous. Payne did."

Not many who were there that day did forget. It happened like this:

Payne, the itinerant missionary, arrived in Mansfield and soon an informal congregation gathered around to hear him preach. An anomaly of the frontier was the willingness of pioneers to stop their work in order to listen to a traveling preacher; similar, in a way, to the philosophers of ancient Athens.

This particular sermon from the long-winded Payne dwelt tediously on the subject of sinful extravagance. Evidently, Payne did not pause to consider that extravagance was a sin in which frugal, hard-working pioneers were not particularly inclined to fall into. The lecture was frequently punctuated with the rhetorical question, "Where now is the primitive Christian, traveling to heaven bare-footed and clad in course raiment?" After this question had been repeated beyond the scope of reasonable endurance, Chapman stood up from the log on which he had been sitting and walked over to where Payne was speaking. Placing his famous bare foot on the stump which Payne had been using as a soap-box, Chapman pointed to his own course raiment and said for all to hear, "Here's your primitive Christian!" They are still laughing there to this day.

The parallel is surprisingly appropriate. John the Baptist was the primitive christian living in the dessert on locusts and wild honey, clad in camel-hair and calling people to repentance. Change a few words, and one has a picture of John Chapman. Many have compared the two Johns. They were both known as "the voice of one crying in the wilderness, make ready the way of the Lord, make His paths straight!"

As for Adam Payne, he later turned up in Illinois where the Indians murdered him, chopped off his head, and touted it as a trophy atop a pole.

Elizabeth Chapman Daughter of Nathanael Chapman and
Elizabeth Chapman Born at Leominster November y 18th 1770
John Chapman Son of Nathanael and Elizabeth Chapman
Born at Leominster September y 26th 1774
Nathanael Chapman Son of Nath.l & Elizabeth Chapman Born
at Leominster June y 26th 1776

A TRUE COPY ATTEST
*George H. Lewis*
City Clerk
City of Leominster

John Chapman (Johnny Appleseed) Birth Certificate

## John Chapman's birth certificate
*City Clerk's Office, Leominster, Mass.*

Mr Martin Mason Sir please
to let Elder Mier or bearer have
thirty Eight apple trees and you will
oblige your friend
John Chapman
Richland Co Ohio
August the 21st 1818

## Reproduction of a tree order, 1818
*Johnny Appleseed Museum, Urbana, OH*

John Chapman order for 150 apple trees, c. 1820
*Johnny Appleseed Museum, Urbana, OH*

Land contract in which Chapman purchases 145 acres in Knox County, OH, for $30
*Johnny Appleseed Museum, Urbana, OH*

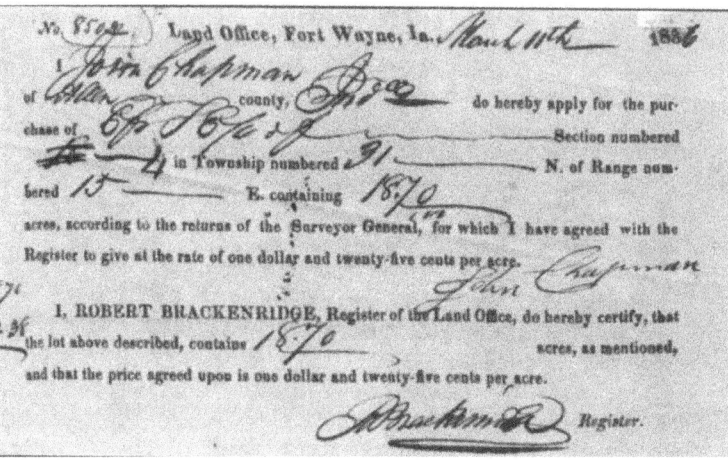

Application for land, 1836
*Records of General Land Office, National Archives*

The Mansfield Blockhouse of 1812

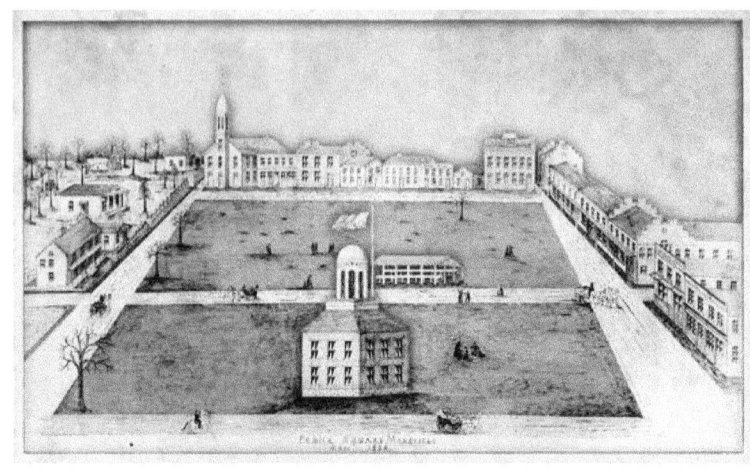

Mansfield Square, OH, 1830

Public Square, Mansfield, OH, 1847
*Historical Collections of Ohio by Henry Howe*

"THE TRIBES OF THE HEATHEN ARE ROUND ABOUT YOUR DOORS, AND A DEVOURING FLAME FOLLOWETH AFTER THEM."

Illustrations of John Chapman, popularizing
the Johnny Appleseed image
*Harper's New Monthly Magazine, November, 1871*

*Engraving in Knapp's History... of Ashland County, 1863, said to have been drawn in the 1850's.*

*Derived from previous engraving. Printed in A. A. Graham's History of Richland County, Ohio, 1880*

John Chapman's gravestone
*Inscription reads: "Johnny Appleseed," John Chapman, He lived for others. 1774-1845*

*Chapter 5*

# Put Your Hand to the Plow

By 1814, Chapman had been planting and maintaining orchards for sixteen of his forty years. During that time, he routinely squatted on unclaimed land, of which there was an abundance. On other occasions, he was a squatter on land that was claimed but unoccupied. These tracts of land would be his home for several weeks as he built a small shelter for himself and planted his orchard.

Whether or not he bothered to obtain a spoken agreement with the landowner before planting is, of course, unknowable. He occasionally did make an effort to obtain land the legal way, but being a kind-hearted and somewhat defenseless man, his claims were often jumped. He subsequently gave up trying to buy land and practiced the much-exercised frontier privilege of squatting for much of his early career.

But by 1814, for reasons known only to himself, Chapman gave up this practice and legally acquired land of his own. The next few years were busy ones for Chapman.

In the spring of the next year, he had lifetime leases on 640 acres of land in Ohio and owned outright two Mount Vernon town lots. According to the terms of the leases, Chapman had to erect cabins on four locations, which were a good distance apart, and make twelve acres tillable in two years. On top of this, interest payments were expected in a few short years, which necessitated that the land not only be tillable, but also bring in a significant income.

While his extensive traveling was necessarily diminished, Chapman's responsibilities vastly increased. Few folks ever accused Chapman of being lazy, with one notable exception. It seems S. C. Coffinbury happened upon Chapman lying on his side under the shade of a tree. As Chapman reclined, he leisurely removed any weed within reach of his hoe. It is one of the few times we ever see him resting.

John Chapman set about building a cabin and clearing land with the same energy and fervor that marked his apple-tree planting expeditions. Never one to do the minimum, Chapman planted a nursery that would later be the patriarch of many large orchards in the nearby counties.

While he was building his cabin, Chapman lived in a primitive lean-to, which was a step up from the hollow logs he was in the habit of using. He worked all day clearing the woods, sowing seeds, and fencing in the area with the trees he had felled. On top of that, his entire subsistence during this time was corn mush. There was nothing of the pleasant, romantic, listless image of Johnny Appleseed in these endeavors. One local boy from Mansfield discovered this the hard way when he volunteered to help Chapman clear some land. It was not the hard work so much as the corn mush that discouraged the boy beyond his limited powers of endurance. He quit after one day.

Two other boys also got an intimate look into Chapman's spartan lifestyle. In 1819, the Vandorn boys made the journey from Washington Township following a line of blazed trees to help Chapman raise logs for a cabin. They found him miles away from anyone and cheerfully surrounded by the usual assortment of dangers and wild animals.

The Vandorns had brought venison, bread, and butter. Chapman took a stick and pulled out some of the potatoes he had cooking in the fire, saying, "This is the way I live in the wilderness."

"Well," one of the boys replied, "you appear to be as happy as a king."

"Yes," said Chapman, "I could not enjoy myself better anywhere - I can lay on my back, look up at the stars and it seems almost as though I can see the angels praising God, for he has made all things for good."

Chapman provided much of the after-dinner conversation with a story about Indian massacres which probably played a part in the sleepless night the Vandorn boys were about to endure. After awhile, they grew tired and dozed off with their feet to the fire. The night sounds of the woods began to bubble into their consciousness. First they heard a wolf pack howling; a sound that is terrifying enough when one is asleep indoors, let alone, outside under a lean-to. The boys jumped up and grabbed their rifles, but Chapman said, "Lay still! They won't hurt you; I am used to them."

"Used to the devil," one of the Vandorns said, "who could be used to such howling and screeching?"

"I like to hear it," said John.

"Well, I suppose you are collogued with the devil," he replied...

"Tut, tut!" said John. "Lay down and go to sleep."

"Well, sleep yourself if you can," said Vandorn, "for I can't."

By that time, Chapman was practically asleep again. After what must have seemed like hours, the Vandorns fitfully dozed off again only to be rudely awakened by an owl directly above their heads. Thinking of Indians, the Vandorns were again on their feet, rifles in hand. "Oh, do let me sleep," Chapman said, "It's nothing but owls – I like to hear them hoot." He rolled over and promptly went back to sleep.

The Vandorn boys should have been prepared for something unusual when they went to help Chapman. After all, it was not the first time they met him. When the Vandorn family moved to Richland County in 1814, Chapman was one of the first frontiersmen to introduce himself. It was Chapman's practice to make friends quickly with new arrivals, help them in some way, and let them know of his apple trees. This was as much a matter of good business sense as it was a spontaneous act of goodwill. On the occasion when he met the Vandorns, Chapman brought with him some medicinal herbs as a housewarming gift.

"After talking about his nurseries and relating some of his wild wood scenes, encounters with rattlesnakes, bears and wolves, he changed the conversation and introduced the subject of Swedenborg; at the same time he began to fumble in his bosom and brought forth some three or four old half-worn-out books. As we were fond of reading, we soon grabbed them, which pleased Johnny. I could see his eyes twinkle with delight. He was much rejoiced to see us eager to read them... When bedtime arrived, Johnny was invited to turn in, a bed being prepared for his especial accommodation, but Johnny declined the proffered kindness, saying he chose to lay on the hearth by the fire, as he did not expect to sleep in a bed in the next world, so he would not in this." Especially in his younger days, he would often forego even the sheltering roof of some friendly cabin. Instead, he would sleep in a hammock strung up between two trees; something he said he learned from the Indians.

"In a time and a place where mass communication was nonexistent and local newspapers still rare, just about everyone seems to have known John Chapman... Stories of him floated from cabin to cabin, from village to village, just as he did."

Though his relation to the land had somewhat changed, Chapman was always the primitive christian, wandering the settlements, planting apple seeds, and bringing "news right fresh from heaven." Hospitable and neighborly; eccentric, but always ready to lend a helping hand to a family in need.

The amount of land he was able to acquire shows that Chapman was not the penniless traveler legends make him out to be. Over the course of his life, he established a thriving nursery business with which he acquired enough money to purchase and lease hundreds of acres. We know that he paid more than $689.76 for sections of land, not counting what he paid out on leases. The destitute image we have today may have been partly a result of his shrewdness in not talking openly about his small fortune.

This was not the only method he had for keeping his money safe. An early biographer wrote, "At one time while contemplating a change in location, having some money on hand, he was afraid the Indians would steal from him (yet had no fear of personal injury) he hid his money under the roots of a large tree where the ground had caved away from the roots. He crawled under the roots and secreted his treasure there. It remained there for three years. He finally returned and found it all safe; at another time he climbed up the comb of the roof of his cabin and stuck his money under the clapboards in such a way as to hide it from view. It remained there for over one year all safe upon his return."

"Few people at one end of these later travels seem ever to have learned much about his business affairs at the other. Nobody beside himself ever knew the full extent of his property. When he died, even his administrators never managed to list all the real estate he still held. And along the trails between his chief centers of visitation, people found out far less. Not letting the right hand know what the left was doing was only Yankee caution. And permitting great numbers of people along his paths to feel that he was an innocent eccentric to whom money was a rarity was sensible perhaps, considering the sums that he transported from time to time and the lonely ways he traveled."

For all his shrewdness in making and protecting money, he gave generously for the furtherance of his faith, and never became miserly or reclusive. He was constantly sociable, hospitable, and generous. He often gave away money, and was even known to use his apple seeds as currency.

Seeds were often more valuable than money on the frontier, and out of his generous nature, "He would give them away to those who could not pay for them. Generally, however, he sold them for old clothing or a supply of corn meal; but he preferred to receive a note payable at some indefinite period. When this was accomplished he seemed to think that the transaction was completed in a business-like way; but if the giver of the note did not attend to its payment, the holder of it never troubled himself about its collection... he was frequently in possession of more money than he cared to keep, and it was quickly disposed of for wintering infirm horses, or given to some poor family whom the ague had prostrated or the accidents of border life impoverished."

Despite the substantial amount of money he acquired over the years, it was never his primary concern. "One morning after he had spent the night on the Slocum's cabin floor, Mr. Slocum found a five-dollar note near where he had slept. He immediately sought out Chapman in town to return it. John examined his pockets carefully, decided the money was really his own, but remonstrated because Slocum had taken the trouble to look him up."

"He never liked to have a (promissory) note dated for a specific day, for, said he, it might not be convenient to collect that day, or it might not be convenient for the customer to pay on that date. He never asked a man to pay a debt, for he reasoned that if God wanted him to have the money, He would move the customer to pay. Besides, the customer knew that he owed the money, without being reminded of it."

By 1823, his leases had played out. Chapman was unable to fulfill all the necessary requirements on his numerous properties and still make enough money from the orchard yields to pay interest on his loans. So at almost fifty years old, he returned to large-scale wanderings. Whether his restlessness was out of a sense of urgency that his time was running out, out of necessity, or out of a love for the simple, wandering life, is lost to time. Regardless, John Chapman was about to embark on his final journey.

*Chapter 6*

# The Valley of the Shadow of Death

John Chapman began his life as an itinerant apple tree planter in 1798. By 1814, he changed his wandering and squatting lifestyle to a more settled one, buying and tending land in Ohio. If his idea had been to rest, he didn't get much of it, as most of his time was spent clearing trees, tilling the ground, and building cabins. Like his missionary work and widespread orchard planting, he threw himself into the task at hand with good-natured energy and industry. But within ten years, payments which he couldn't afford were required on his numerous tracts of land and some 160 acres were forfeited. The sizable land venture he had started in 1814 ran dry, and so in 1823, Chapman returned to a nomadic lifestyle. "It is difficult to believe that he profited much from the investment as a whole. At the age of forty-nine, his chief assets still consisted of his nurseries, his freedom of action, and his seemingly limitless endurance."

In a day when the average life expectancy hovered around thirty-five to forty years of age, it might have been assumed that his best and most prodigious years of work were behind him. In fact, just the opposite was true. Like his apple trees, Chapman improved with age.

He began pushing further west into Indiana, and established a truly immense string of nurseries which he would continue to grow and tend till his death. Just how far west Chapman went is speculative, though it is quite certain that he did not plant any orchards in California, despite at least one claim to the contrary. Ridiculous as it is, it demonstrates the expanse of the Appleseed legend. Indiana was probably the westernmost extent of Chapman's journeys.

While his lifestyle had, in some ways, reverted to what it had been before he bought the sections of land in Ohio, there was one habit he retained from those years; he was now reluctant to plant trees without a written lease from the owner. This proved a safer, though more expensive, mode of operation. Chapman quickly found that he had to pay anywhere from sixty dollars to one thousand apple trees for the right to plant on a piece of land. For the rest of his life, he moved across Ohio to Ft. Wayne and back. In the spring, he went west, returning east in late summer.

Also during this period of his life, he was known to make more extensive use of rivers in transporting himself and his seeds. An eyewitness reported seeing Chapman in the fall of 1830, paddling up the Maumee River in a portion of a hollowed out tree and docking in Fort Wayne. He was also seen in a canoe distributing apple trees on the Blanchard River in Ohio.

By now, Chapman's largest nursery was about a mile north of the town of Defiance, Ohio. He is said to have lived in the thirteen foot hollow of an old sycamore tree while tending this nursery. The nursery reportedly sprouted several thousand seedlings in the early 1830s and became the father of at least four other nurseries.

Just as Chapman hadn't been the first to introduce apple trees to North America, so he was also not the first to introduce them to the Ohio-Indiana area. French traders had planted a few sporadic trees that were still in existence in Chapman's day, thanks to careful tending from Indians and trappers. One of these ancient giants stood near

Defiance measuring nine feet in diameter, forty-five feet high, and producing two hundred bushels (1,600 gallons) of apples a year.

During most of his life, Ohio and the Mansfield area in particular, were as close to a home base as Chapman ever had. Aside from his first appearance in Pennsylvania and the occasional trips he made back to replenish his apple seeds, Ohio was where he spent most of his time planting, building, serving, and doing missionary work. But that, too, was about to change.

From 1834 to 1838, Chapman bought large sections of land again, this time in Indiana. He worked the land on a semi-regular basis, and some suggest that this time, he was preparing to settle down for good. Indiana became his new base of operations, though he still returned to central Ohio in the summer to pick up more apple seeds and tend his nurseries.

His lifestyle continued much as it had decades earlier. He traveled the frontier, spending the night in the woods or a friendly cabin where he would talk of God and Swedenborg. He carried no gun, wore no shoes, had no home, didn't sleep in a bed or kill an animal, and wore nothing but an unsightly patchwork of ragged clothes. Few, indeed, would ever have suspected that this wandering planter of apple trees had owned, over the course of his life, almost twelve hundred acres of land.

As for his personality, that didn't change, either. One acquaintance said, "I once saw him most outrageously abused by a man much smaller than himself... for some offense he had unwittingly committed. After reviling him in the hardest language, he kicked him, all which John bore with great meekness, and totally unruffled, and if he had been struck on one cheek, he would have turned the other."

Despite his age, he was still willing to help anyone in need. "(A)t one time was invited to a house raising, to which he went, hoping to be of some use on this as well as other occasions. In the act of carrying a log, he espied a house on fire in the distance. "Fire!" said he and dropped the log; he started off at full speed, his companions (about forty of them) followed suit. Johnny was then sixty-eight years old and yet he outran the whole of them, arriving at the burning building first."

Chapman also had a new nursery in Indiana that rivaled even the one in Defiance. By 1845, the year Chapman died, his 42 acres of land north of the Maumee River produced somewhere in the neighborhood of fifteen thousand apple trees. The single largest tree he is said to have planted, was reported to reach a circumference of ninety-two inches, slightly over seven and a half feet.

Chapman visited Ohio for the last time around 1842.

From the time John Chapman first reached the Allegheny Plateau to the time he died, thriving cities and towns had emerged all over the northern counties of Ohio where he did most of his work. The frontier wilderness that Chapman had known and the pioneers among whom he lived were disappearing as canals, railroads, farms, and houses took their place. What had once been the Wild West, where only Indians and trappers ventured, was now being civilized into an ever-growing population of town and city dwellers. In a very real sense, John Chapman had hastened this civilization. His apple orchards paved the way for settlers and their families to come and thrive, and his uncanny ability to predict the next burst of western expansion greatly increased the speed with which settlement was able to take place. The rapidly-changing face of the midwest, and hence all of America, owes its greatest debt of gratitude to John Chapman, perhaps more than to anyone else.

In March 1845, Chapman was working on his land in Indiana when he was told that one of his nurseries on the St. Joseph River near Ft. Wayne had been damaged by cattle. He immediately started off on foot. By the time he arrived, he was very tired and weak from the journey. He rested at the Worth family cabin, but in a few days, fever set in, and on the eighteenth of March, 1845, Chapman entered the heaven on which his eyes were always fixed. He did not die as many did; at home, resting from his labors. For Chapman, there was no home and his labors were never done. "The physician who pronounced him dying later said that he had never seen a man so placid in his final passage."

His body was laid to rest in the March snows, and the ground to which he had always been especially close, received his last remains.

The exact location of his grave is unknown, but "no particular place can adequately memorialize John Chapman, anyhow." He was a unique man. "Chapman had the eye of a speculator, the heart of a philanthropist, the courage of a frontiersman, and the wandering instincts of a Bedouin nomad." An extensive traveler, generous benefactor, kind-hearted servant, fervent missionary, hard-worker, and friendly neighbor. A "medicine man; lord of the open trail, with the stars for a roof and the moon for his night-light; pioneer capitalist; altruist," and so much more. But now it was left to those who remained and who remembered, to carry on his legacy; no longer would the barefoot nurseryman walk the road to Ft. Wayne, or plant apple trees in Ohio. The one whom Harper's Magazine called the "Pioneer Hero" had died.

"But spring would come on the twenty-first, and eighteen days afterward the Andrews weather entry would read: 'In the night thunder showers - then fair - first apple blossoms.' "

*Afterward*

# Children Shall Rise up and Call You Blessed

Of the many eulogies in Chapman's honor, Harper's Magazine's is particularly moving: "Thus died one of the memorable men of pioneer times, who never inflicted pain or knew an enemy - a man of strange habits, in whom there dwelt a comprehensive love that reached with one hand downward to the lowest forms of life, and with the other upward to the very throne of God. A laboring, self-denying benefactor of his race, homeless, solitary, and ragged, he trod the thorny earth with bare and bleeding feet, intent only upon making the wilderness fruitful."

John Chapman's legacy spread from the Allegheny Plateau to Fort Wayne, and far beyond. In planting nurseries, Chapman paved the way for the great western expansion of the early 1800s that would change the face of America economically, politically, and spiritually. The speed with which the midwest was civilized was due, in large part, to Chapman's tireless efforts, and led to the next great rush of manifest destiny that would cover all of continental United States. "In 1800, the population of Ohio was not above 40,000. By 1830, when Johnny moved his base of operations farther west into Indiana, it was almost a million." How much this rise in population is attributable to Chapman, is unknown and unknowable. We do know that hundreds of orchards in Ohio and Indiana derive their lineage from Chapman's nurseries, and the apples we enjoy today may be the great grandchildren of Chapman's original seeds transported from cider presses in Pennsylvania.

His spiritual legacy is equally impressive. Aside from Swedenborg himself, John Chapman is undoubtedly the best-known follower of New Church doctrine and contributed greatly to its presence in the midwest. Many, if not most, of the New Church societies that sprang up in Ohio and Indiana during the 1800s are a direct result of Chapman's evangelistic efforts. While quantifiable numbers are unknown, his constant efforts are tribute enough to his work in bringing a knowledge of the Bible and religion to the west.

In innumerable small, and now forgotten ways, Chapman lent a helping hand to neighbors and families in distress. Whether it was giving money or clothes, helping raise a house or repair a fence, bringing a house-warming gift of medicinal herbs, or helping a family of orphans start their own apple tree business, Chapman was often there to help. Due in large part to his extensive travels and eccentricities, he is one of the most ubiquitous historical characters on the early frontier. There were few settlers who did not know the name John Appleseed and who did not experience either directly, or otherwise, the kind and gentle touch of his hand.

He attached little value to money and financial security, despite being a vast landholder for much of his life. He voluntarily chose a strenuous, nomadic life in order to spread the doctrines of the faith in which he believed. And most of all, there is the sheer vastness of the nurseries he planted and maintained.

Even before he died, Chapman's life had become an inspiration to many. Individualism, kindness, gentleness, spiritual zeal, industry, and disregard for physical suffering are just a few of the principles around which he built his life. Today we think of a barefoot cartoon character with a pot on his head courtesy of Walt Disney who took, shall we say, some artistic liberties.

In many ways, it seems Chapman was made of a different substance than us mortals. What we know of his physical endurance and seemingly boundless energy began when he was twenty-three, on the trek from Massachusetts to Pennsylvania, and continued undiminished till the day he died at seventy years of age. He was generous with his time and resources and gave no thought to himself.

But the real John Chapman was also a man of flesh and blood, just like us. He grew tired and hungry and needed to eat and sleep. He had a sense of humor, and he got into arguments with preachers and trouble with Indians. He told tall tales, often about himself, husked corn, cut down trees, repaired fences, and got stung by bees and bit by snakes.

What sets him apart was that he was, above all, a man who practiced what he preached. He believed in principles and ideas which he followed tenaciously, even at the cost of a good bed, shoes for his feet, and a place he could call home. He built his entire life around what he believed, and as a result, changed the world. To live what we believe; that is a lesson we must remember and follow if we are to truly honor his legacy.

This is who Johnny Appleseed is to me, and as they said, he shall shine as the stars forever.

# Notes:

## Chapter 1: He Shall Be Called John

\* The Revenue Act of 1764, better known as the Sugar Act, put a three-penny tax on every gallon of molasses entering the colonies from outside the British empire. It would later be reduced to one penny.

\*\* This was brought to my attention by Ophia Smith, in *Johnny Appleseed, a Voice in the Wilderness* Third Edition (1947) pg. 45, "The Story of 'Johnny Appleseed' "

"She felt that she" Price, Robert "A Trail from New England", *Johnny Appleseed: Man & Myth*, (Urbana University, Urbana, Ohio, 1954) 13

"By the time" Price, Robert "A Trail from New England", *Johnny Appleseed: Man & Myth*, (Urbana University, Urbana, Ohio, 1954) 15

"last brave letter" Ibid.

"Any boy's inspirations" Price, Robert "A Trail from New England", *Johnny Appleseed: Man & Myth*, (Urbana University, Urbana, Ohio, 1954) 16

\*\*\* The story of the horse-kicking that John allegedly received was famously circulated by W. M. Glines, an acquaintance of Chapman, and is supposed to make sense of John's eccentricities. Glines is not the only person to suggest a reason for John Chapman's peculiarities. Another popular story is that of disappointed love. No single theory is especially convincing.

## Chapter 2: A Time to Plant

"a small man" Coffinbury, S.C. letter to Mansfield *Shield and Banner*, Nov. 23, 1871, reprinted in Mansfield *Ohio Liberal*, Aug. 27, 1873; Henry Newman, letter, March, 1873, in A. A. Graham, *History of Richland County, Ohio* (Mansfield, 1880), 450; E. Bonar McLaughlin, *Pioneer Directory and Scrap Book... of Richland County, Ohio* (Mansfield, 1870), 15

"Generally even in the coldest weather" Harper's New Monthly Magazine, Volume 0043, Issue 258 (November 1871) Title: "Johnny Appleseed - A Pioneer Hero" (page 831) by Haley, W.D.

"he was frequently seen" Coffinbury, S.C. letter to Mansfield *Shield and Banner*, Nov. 23, 1871, reprinted in Mansfield *Ohio Liberal*, Aug. 27, 1873; Henry Newman, letter, March, 1873, in A. A. Graham, *History of Richland County, Ohio* (Mansfield, 1880), 450; E. Bonar McLaughlin, *Pioneer Directory and Scrap Book... of Richland County, Ohio* (Mansfield, 1870), 15

"He slept on the floor" Indiana Horticultural Society, Transactions, XXII, 35-40

"Almost as important" Means, Howard "Right Fresh from Heaven", *Johnny Appleseed: The Man, the Myth, the American Story*, (Simon & Schuster, 2011) 8 "preparing a way" Price, Robert "Apples on the Border", *Johnny Appleseed: Man & Myth*, (Urbana University, Urbana, Ohio, 1954) 43

"He would describe" Harper's New Monthly Magazine, Volume 0043, Issue 258 (November 1871) Title: "Johnny Appleseed - A Pioneer Hero" (page 834) by Haley, W.D.

"no other orchardist" Fortriede, Steven "The Ohio Frontier", *Johnny Appleseed: The Man Behind the Myth* (Fort Wayne Public Library, 1978) 8 & 9

"he denounced as absolute wickedness" Harper's New Monthly Magazine, Volume 0043, Issue 258 (November 1871) Title: "Johnny Appleseed - A Pioneer Hero" (page 834) by Haley, W.D.

"with two canoes lashed together" Harper's New Monthly Magazine, Volume 0043, Issue 258 (November 1871) Title: "Johnny Appleseed - A Pioneer Hero" (page 830) by Haley, W.D.

"All his work was done by hand" Glines, W.M. *Johnny Appleseed by One Who Knew Him*, (Ohio State Archaeological and Historical Society, 1922) 8

"It also appears that" Fortriede, Steven "The Ohio Frontier", *Johnny Appleseed: The Man Behind the Myth* (Fort Wayne Public Library, 1978) 9

\* On March 3, 2014, in the interests of science, the author attempted to thaw ice with his bare feet in temperatures of about fifteen degrees, Fahrenheit. Bundled in winter coat

and gloves, with bare feet alone exposed to the elements, he stood for a little over three minutes on a small pile of ice, after which the pain became too great to bear, even in the interests of science, and the author retreated to the safety and warmth of his house, a luxury not available to Chapman. The amount of thawing was so negligible as to allow only disheartening conclusions. This story about John Chapman is:
a) Untrue
b) A legend invented by some imaginative personage, or else created for effect from his own teeming brain.
c) Chapman's powers of endurance greatly exceed that of his distant posterity.

This last option is doubtless the case. The only question that remains now is whether or not even Chapman's seemingly inexhaustible fortitude was strong enough to engage in the ice-thawing with greater success. At this late date, such a valuable fact is, in all likelihood, unknowable. In any case, the experiment was inconclusive at best, and not recommended.

"he stuck pins in his feet" Means, Howard "Right Fresh from Heaven", Johnny Appleseed, (Simon & Schuster Publishers 2011) 12

"He frequently lived" Glines, W.M. *Johnny Appleseed by One Who Knew Him*, (Ohio State Archaeological and Historical Society, 1922) 11

"On one occasion" Harper's New Monthly Magazine, Volume 0043, Issue 258 (November 1871) Title: "Johnny Appleseed - A Pioneer Hero" (page 831) by Haley, W.D.

## Chapter 3: Standing in the Gates

"He would often examine" Glines, W.M. *Johnny Appleseed by One Who Knew Him*, (Ohio State Archaeological and Historical Society, 1922) 12

"that to leave a mother bear" Price, Robert "Johnny Appleseed in American Folklore and Literature" from *Johnny Appleseed, a Voice in the Wilderness*, Third Edition (The Swedenborg Press, 1947) 7

"He was careful not to injure" Howe, Henry *Historical Collections of Ohio*, 1846

"The Spirit of the Lord" Harper's New Monthly Magazine, Volume 0043, Issue 258 (November 1871) Title: "Johnny Appleseed - A Pioneer Hero" (page 833) by Haley, W.D.

## Chapter 4: A Voice of One in the Wilderness

"devoutly believed that the more" *Fort Wayne Sentinel*, March 22, 1845

"He was a constant reader" Glines, W.M. *Johnny Appleseed by One Who Knew Him*, (Ohio State Archaeological and Historical Society, 1922) 12

"I have sent some books" *Some Letters of William Schlatter 1814 to 1825* (typescript from letter books), New Church Theological School Library, Cambridge, Mass.

"He always carried with him" *Fort Wayne Sentinel*, March 22, 1845

"I have received a letter" *Some Letters of William Schlatter 1814 to 1825* (typescript from letter books), New Church Theological School Library, Cambridge, Mass.

"To add something more" quoted in "The Story of 'Johnny Appleseed'" from *Johnny Appleseed, a Voice in the Wilderness*, Third Edition (The Swedenborg Press, 1947) 50

"one very extraordinary missionary" Journal of the Proceedings of the Fifth General Convention of the Receivers of the Doctrines of the New Jerusalem, Philadelphia, June 3, 1822, 7

"Never has there been such" Price, Robert "A Very Extraordinary Missionary", *Johnny Appleseed: Man & Myth*, (Urbana University, Urbana, Ohio, 1954) 136

"He believed this world" Price, Robert "The Folk Tales Grow", *Johnny Appleseed: Man & Myth*, (Urbana University, Urbana, Ohio, 1954) 176-177

"Of all Johnny Appleseed's actual" Price, Robert "The Folk Tales Grow", *Johnny Appleseed: Man & Myth*, (Urbana University, Urbana, Ohio, 1954) 177-178

"the voice of one" Matthew 3:3. Scripture quotations taken from the New American Standard Bible® (NASB), Copyright © 1960, 1962, 1963, 1968, 1971, 1972,

1973, 1975, 1977, 1995 by The Lockman Foundation. Used by permission. www.Lockman.org

## Chapter 5: Put Your Hand to the Plow

Dialog taken from a letter by E. Vandorn to the "Ohio Liberal", August 13, 20, 1873

"After talking about" from a letter by E. Vandorn to the "Ohio Liberal", August 13, 20, 1873

"In a time and a place" Means, Howard "Right Fresh from Heaven", Johnny Appleseed, (Simon & Schuster Publishers 2011) 11

"At one time while contemplating" Glines, W.M. *Johnny Appleseed by One Who Knew Him*, (Ohio State Archaeological and Historical Society, 1922) 11-12

"Few people at one end" Price, Robert "Last Journeys", *Johnny Appleseed: Man & Myth*, (Urbana University, Urbana, Ohio, 1954) 223-224

"He would give them away" Harper's New Monthly Magazine, Volume 0043, Issue 258 (November 1871) Title: "Johnny Appleseed - A Pioneer Hero" (page 835) by Haley, W.D.

"One morning after he" Price, Robert "The Folk Tales Grow", *Johnny Appleseed: Man & Myth*, (Urbana University, Urbana, Ohio, 1954) 173

"He never liked to have" Smith, Ophia "The Story of 'Johnny Appleseed'" from *Johnny Appleseed, a Voice in the Wilderness*, Third Edition (The Swedenborg Press, 1947) 53

## Chapter 6: The Valley of the Shadow of Death

"It is difficult to believe" Price, Robert "Portrait at Fifty", *Johnny Appleseed: Man & Myth*, (Urbana University, Urbana, Ohio, 1954) 155-156

"I once saw him" Price, Robert "Last Journeys", *Johnny Appleseed: Man & Myth*, (Urbana University, Urbana, Ohio, 1954) 211

"at one time was invited" Price, Robert "A Time to Die", *Johnny Appleseed: Man & Myth*, (Urbana University, Urbana, Ohio, 1954) 233

"The physician who" Means, Howard "Right Fresh from Heaven", *Johnny Appleseed: The Man, the Myth, the American Story*, (Simon & Schuster, 2011) 2

"no particular place" Price, Robert "A Time to Die", *Johnny Appleseed: Man & Myth*, (Urbana University, Urbana, Ohio, 1954) 237

"Chapman had the" Means, Howard "Right Fresh from Heaven", *Johnny Appleseed: The Man, the Myth, the American Story*, (Simon & Schuster, 2011) 9 "medicine man" Means, Howard "Right Fresh from Heaven", *Johnny Appleseed: The Man, the Myth, the American Story*, (Simon & Schuster, 2011) 4

"But spring would come" Price, Robert "A Time to Die", *Johnny Appleseed: Man & Myth*, (Urbana University, Urbana, Ohio, 1954) 240

## Afterward: Children Shall Rise up and Call You Blessed

"Thus died one of the memorable men" Harper's New Monthly Magazine, Volume 0043, Issue 258 (November 1871) Title: "Johnny Appleseed - A Pioneer Hero" (page 836) by Haley, W.D.

"In 1800, the population" Fortriede, Steven "The Ohio Frontier", *Johnny Appleseed: The Man Behind the Myth* (Fort Wayne Public Library, 1978) 7

# A Note on the Type

This book is set in Baskerville, designed in 1757 by John Baskerville and cut by John Handy. A contemporary said of Baskerville, "You would be a means of blinding all the readers of the nation, for the strokes of your letters being too thin and narrow, hurt the eye." I have chosen Baskerville for its historic value, as it was likely used to produce reams of revolutionary propaganda in Paris during the reign of terror, and because I can't afford to license Doves, the most historic, beautiful, and prestigious of all serifs.

www.ingramcontent.com/pod-product-compliance
Lightning Source LLC
Chambersburg PA
CBHW050543300426
44113CB00012B/2242